MYSTERY

of the

MISSING PEAS

Written by Tessa Greene

Illustrated by Shannon Vogus

Cover illustration by Shannon Vogus

Cover design by Anna Asfour

© 2021 Jenny Phillips

goodandbeautiful.com

Challenge Words:

grew

garden

groundhog

mystery

clue

what

Billy and Ella loved to garden.

Every day, Billy and Ella went
in the garden to pull weeds and
water their plants.

Billy and Ella grew
all sorts of plants
in their garden!

They grew beans...

corn...

and carrots.

They really loved peas!

Billy and Ella took good care of their peas.

On warm days Billy and Ella liked to pick some peas to share.

Peas are round, small, green, and yummy!

One sunny day, Billy and Ella went into the garden to take care of their plants.

They hoped there would be a big pod of peas there for them.

But when Billy and Ella got to the garden, they found that some of their peas were gone!

"Oh, no!" said Ella. "Who would do such a thing?"

"I'm not sure," said Billy, "but we will find out. We have a mystery!"

"What do we
do?" asked Ella.

"Well, first I think we have to look for clues," said Billy.

So Billy and Ella started to look for clues.
They walked around their pea plants.

They walked all over the garden.

They looked all over the
yard! But they did not
see anything odd.

"It's okay, Ella," said Billy. "We can look for more clues later."

The next day, Billy and Ella went
back to the garden to look for clues.
Even more peas were gone!

"Oh, no!" said Billy.
"Come on, Ella. What
can we find?"

"Billy," said Ella. She was looking at the ground. "What do clues look like?"

"They can look like all sorts of things," said Billy.

"Is that a clue?" asked Ella.
There were animal tracks!

"Maybe an animal is taking our peas," said Ella.

"That must be it!" Billy said.
"Come on. I have an idea."

Ella went with Billy and found
some sticks and rope.

"We can use these to
make a wall," said Billy.

Billy and Ella spent all day making
a wall around their peas.

"There," Billy said when they were done. "No animals can get to our peas now."

The next day, Billy and Ella looked at their peas again. "Oh, no!" said Ella. "There are more gone!"

All that was left was one pod of peas on the plant.

"Hold on, what is that?" asked Ella. Billy looked behind the pea plants.

They looked closer. Then, a little nose poked out of the hole!

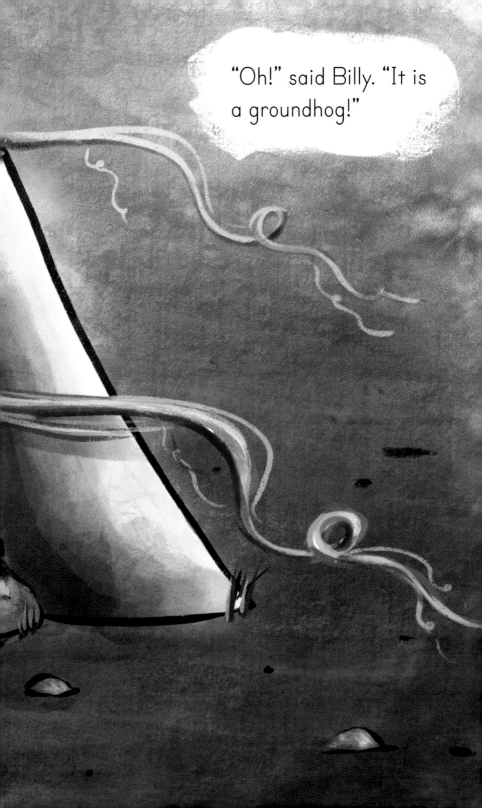

Ella smiled. "That must be who is taking our peas!

"Not all of them!"
said Ella.

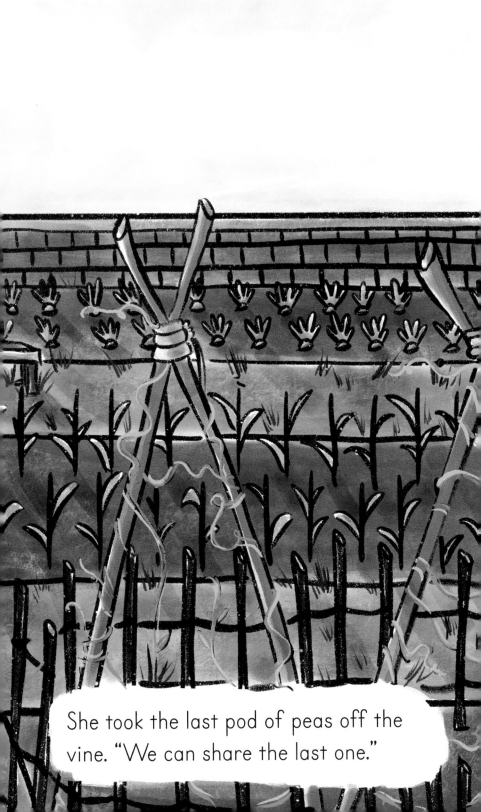

She took the last pod of peas off the vine. "We can share the last one."

Billy and Ella opened the pod, and they each ate half of the peas.

Ella said, "It tastes good
to solve a mystery!"

Check out these other Level I books from The Good and the Beautiful!

Dave and the Frog
by Jenny Phillips

Josh Gets a Bird
by Joseph Wiseman and
Heather Wiseman